Hanne Bloch

GRAND-MOTHER'S
cooking

Traditional Danish Dishes

Komma & Clausen

Front cover: A fine Sunday dinner is served: roast beef with a thick layer of crispy fat, glazed onions, and fixings. And for dessert there is lemon mousse with whipped cream. See pages 58 and 50.

ISBN 87-7512-593-5

Hanne Bloch: GRANDMOTHER'S COOKING -
Traditional Danish Dishes, translated by
Martha Gaber Abrahamsen from MORMORS KØKKEN -
traditionelle danske retter.
Copyright © 1992 Komma & Clausen Bøger A/S
Emdrupvej 28 C, DK-2100 København Ø.

Lay-out by S.C.Sejersen reklame A/S, Viborg
Printed by Specialtrykkeriet, Viborg
Photos: Peter Kam
Cover lay-out: Bent Juul Nielsen
Editor: Kirsten Corvinius

CONTENTS

CONVERSION TABLE

Any cook who enjoys making food from different countries probably has different kinds of measuring cups. It is a good idea to buy cups or pitchers for measuring deciliters if you intend to use Continental recipes. Or mark off 1 and 2 deciliters on a glass measuring cup. The recipes in this cookbook use simple measurements, so conversion will be no problem. Here are a few guidelines with approximate equivalents that can be used in all these recipes:

Weights
1 kilogram (kg) = 1000 grams = just over 2 pounds
1 pound = 16 ounces = just under 500 grams (g)
100 g = 3.5 ounces
1 ounce = just under 30 grams

Measures
1 quart = just under 1 liter = nearly 10 deciliters (dl)
1 U.S. cup = 8 fluid ounces = 2 ¼ dl
1 British cup = 10 fluid ounces = nearly 3 dl

Standard measuring teaspoons and tablespoons can be used for all recipes.

Approximate oven temperatures

	°Centigrade	°Fahrenheit
Very slow	125-135	250-275
Slow	150-175	300-325
Moderate	175-200	350-375
Hot	200-225	400-425
Very hot	225-250	450-475

Gelatin is available in leaves (thin sheets) in much of Europe. One envelope of unflavored gelatin thickens 2 ¼ dl of liquid and equals 4-5 gelatin leaves. Dissolve the gelatin powder in a little water before using as directed for gelatin leaves.

Vanilla extract can be substituted for vanilla pods. Add the vanilla extract after the liquid has been taken from the heat.

GRANDMOTHER'S COOKING

TRADITIONAL DANISH FOOD

An old-fashioned joint of beef covered with crispy fat, meatballs as only mother knew how to make them, pork roast with crackling, salted brisket of beef with cabbage, red berry soup, vanilla ice cream - these are a few of the foods from our childhood which we will always remember as something very special. Mother and grandmother prepared them regularly, following recipes that had been handed down for generations.

French finesses, Italian pasta and pizza specialties, heat-and-serve dishes, and fast food have to some extent supplanted the Danish beef patties with onions, but this is often just the kind of food we dream of. Who can resist a portion of hot elderberry soup with apples or stewed beef with mashed potatoes when it's cold outside? And what is a summer without red berry soup with cream?

I clearly remember almond pudding with red cherry sauce from my childhood, but how do you make it? This cookbook gives recipes for traditional Danish dishes that I enjoyed at home as a child, dishes which my own family still eats. Many Danish dishes have naturally been influenced from abroad throughout the ages, adapted to our climate, temperament, and way of life. Greasy or thick sauces are often associated with old Danish cooking, and for good reason I have left them out since times and eating habits have changed. Today we want lighter, simpler food, and our work today does not require the same calorie-rich meals that were necessary a generation or two ago.

Even though the season for many ingredients is not as clearly defined as it once was, there are still - luckily - seasonal ingredients. The first new Danish potatoes are still a special treat, and so is a compote prepared from the first delicate rhubarb stalks. And of course there are sugared red currants, for me, the epitome of the Danish summer.

Good ingredients are always the first requirement when we want to put a good meal on the table. Our grandmothers knew this, and we know it today, even though we often let ourselves be tempted by the easy way out and throw quality to the winds. I wonder if most of us know that you need proper meat to make even an ordinary meatball. Keep this in mind and you will get the most out of this book.

Hanne Bloch

SPRING

(March - April - May)

Even though the first spring month can be icy cold, you can almost hear the buds getting ready to open. There is more light, and we naturally also choose lighter dishes. Easter time means eggs, and Danish dishes include eggs in mustard sauce, always a good spring and Easter treat. Danish omelet, or egg cake, with plenty of finely clipped chives is served the year round, but for our grandparents, it was reserved for spring, when the hens began to lay eggs again after the long winter. The first delicate rhubarb stems can be found at the grocer's in April and May, and tempt us to make compotes or fruit soup. And the fish and game store has bunches of newly shot rooks side by side with spring bucks. Modern technology is still not able to control the natural occurrences of fish. When the seas get a bit warmer around us, mackerel and garfish are caught, and if the weather permits, there are shrimp from Denmark's fjords in May.

CHERVIL SOUP
SERVES 4

Chervil can be found at the grocer's in early spring, fresh-grown in pots or cut and sealed in plastic envelopes. The young leaves and stems are used. Fresh chervil should always be added last to the soup so that its taste, color, and vitamins are retained. And in early spring, we especially need vitamin C, which is found in abundance in chervil.

c. 150 g fresh chervil
1 ¼ liter stock made from veal
and/or pork bones
4 carrots
2-3 leeks

4 tbsp. butter
4 tbsp. flour
salt and pepper
Accompaniments: Halved boiled
eggs (not too hard)

Rinse the chervil well and chop it finely. Scrape the carrots and slice thinly. Clean, rinse, and slice the leeks. Cook the carrots and leeks until tender in the stock. Cream the butter and flour until smooth and beat the mixture into the stock. Boil the soup for a few minutes and mix in the freshly chopped chervil. Heat briefly and season with salt and pepper. Do not let the soup boil again or it will lose its lovely green color. Add halved boiled eggs to the soup or serve on the side.

Hint: You can add little meatballs to chervil soup just before serving, and pieces of cooked asparagus can be used instead of leek.

SEVEN-VEGETABLE SOUP
SERVES 4

The recipe is found in old cookbooks and was probably best known and used most often in the country, where it was easier to get the green ingredients. The soup was made at Easter time from 7 different kinds of vegetables. In order to use the magical number 7 the cook had to have plenty of imagination, so both fresh nettles and gooseberry leaves were often used for the soup. The basic stock was made from a good hen. Here we have used a pullet instead.

1 meaty pullet (young hen)	4-5 kale leaves
1 tbsp. salt	½ kg fresh spinach
2 liters water	a handful of fresh chervil
2 carrots	a handful of fresh nettle leaves
2 leeks	a bunch of parsley
¼ celeriac	a bunch of dill
bouquet garni of leek and	a bunch of chives
celeriac leaves	

Place the dressed pullet in a pot and cover with water. Bring to a boil and skim the surface. Add salt and carrots, cut into pieces. Cut the green part off the leeks, slice them finely, and reserve until later. Add the rest of the leeks to the soup together with the sliced celeriac and bouquet garni. Cover and simmer gently until the pullet is done, a little more than an hour. Remove the pullet and sieve the soup. Pour it back into the pot and add the finely sliced leek tops. Rinse and chop the other greens. Add them to the soup and heat. Season with salt and pepper. Cut the pullet into serving pieces and serve with the soup together with whole-grained bread.

Hint: Use celery instead of celeriac. Then add the finely chopped leaves last. Finely sliced Chinese cabbage can be added to the soup and replace or supplement the greens added last.

FJORD SHRIMP

The fjord shrimp, or Roskilde shrimp, is the smallest variety found in Denmark. This little brownish-gray shrimp is caught from late spring to far into the summer. Depending on wind and weather, the catches are either big or small, and prices vary accordingly. As a rule, the fjord shrimp is cheapest just before the Tivoli Gardens open. Fjord shrimp is sold live. It is quite a job - but not impossible - to shell these little creatures, which is why they are so expensive when they are bought ready cooked and shelled.

Cooking and serving fjord shrimp

Allow ¼ kg fresh shrimp per person.
2 tsp. salt per liter water
a bunch of dill

Bring the lightly salted water to a boil. Add the fresh shrimp and boil briefly. Remove the pot from the stove immediately and let the shrimp stand in the liquid before serving. It is easiest to shell the shrimp when they are warm. They taste best when they are not too cold.
To serve: Each person shells his own portion. Serve with fresh bread, butter, and lemon.
"Shrimp in a crowd": Place a heap of shelled fjord shrimp on buttered white bread. Garnish with lemon wedges.

DEEP-FRIED FJORD SHRIMP
SERVES 4

1 kg unshelled shrimp
For deep frying:
1 liter oil or 1 kg unseasoned fat

Accompaniments:
Lemon, dill, bread

Rinse the shrimp and drain well in a sieve. If necessary, dry them a bit on paper towels. Heat the fat in a pot with a thick bottom. Deep-fry the shrimp, a little portion at a time, until they just turn pink. Remove the shrimp with a slotted spoon and drain on absorbent paper. Serve immediately with lemon wedges, dill sprigs, and bread.

EGGS IN MUSTARD SAUCE
SERVES 4

Eggs in mustard sauce was a common dish at Easter time or when the family had to cut down on expensive meat. Here we use lightly salted pork, while lightly salted or smoked pork fat was used in olden days.

8 eggs
½ kg lightly salted pork
(for boiling or roasting)
4 tbsp. butter
4 tbsp. flour

1-2 tbsp. mustard
(depending on the strength)
½ liter milk
salt and pepper
a bunch of chives

Boil the eggs for only 7 minutes. Shell. Cut the pork into slices or small cubes. Brown them on a frying pan. Melt the butter and cream it with the flour. Thin with milk and cook the sauce for a few minutes. Mix in the mustard and season with salt and pepper. Add the shelled eggs and heat the sauce. Do not let the sauce boil after the mustard has been added or it will get bitter. Pour into a deep platter and sprinkle on finely clipped chives. Serve the pork slices on the side or sprinkle on pork cubes just before the chives.
Variation: Leave out the mustard and instead add 3-4 tbsp. grated cheese to the sauce together with 1 chopped, browned onion and browned pork cubes. Put the sauce into a baking dish and sprinkle with a mixture of dried bread crumbs and cheese. Gratinate for 5-10 minutes at 225°C.

FRIED MARCKEREL WITH GOOSEBERRY SAUCE
SERVES 4

Mackerel is one variety we consider spring fish, even though it is meatier later on in the year. But if you serve fried mackerel with gooseberry sauce, it's as if summer were just around the corner.

2-3 fresh mackerels
salt and pepper
3 tbsp. flour
1 lemon
fat for frying

Gooseberry Sauce:
250 g green (unripe) gooseberries
3 dl water, 3 tbsp. sugar
3 tbsp. butter
1 ½ tbsp. flour
salt and pepper

Gut and rinse the fish and dredge in a mixture of flour, salt, and pepper. Cut the fish into serving pieces. First brown the fish on both sides in fat. Then lower the heat and fry the fish 5-6 minutes on each side. Sprinkle with lemon juice during frying to add taste and reduce the fishy odor in the kitchen.

Gooseberry Sauce: Pick over and rinse the gooseberries. Cook them in a pot with the water and sugar for 10 minutes or until tender. Press them through a sieve. Return the purée to the pot. Cream the butter and flour and whisk the mixture into the gooseberry purée. Boil briefly and season with salt and pepper. Serve the fried mackerel with boiled potatoes and gooseberry sauce.

Variation: Gut and rinse the mackerels, cut into serving pieces, and fill them with parsley. Hold the pieces together with thread or toothpicks. Dredge them in flour, salt, and pepper, and fry. Serve with parsley sauce instead of gooseberry sauce.

FRIED GARFISH FILLED WITH PARSLEY
SERVES 4

The fish with the green bones can be bought deboned today. Your fish dealer has special tongs for the purpose and it is easy to have the whole backbone removed at one time. The garfish is one of the lean varieties caught in Danish waters from the end of April. Fried garfish and garfish in aspic were familiar dishes 50 years ago and still are today.

2 fresh garfish, 1 ½ kg in all   salt and pepper
1 medium onion   butter for frying
2-3 bunches of parsley
1 egg   *Sauce:* 50 g butter
1 dl dried bread crumbs   vinegar

Let your fish dealer debone the garfish if the family wants to avoid the green bones. Personally I think the fish has more flavor with the bones in. Cut the fish into serving pieces. Peel and dice the onion and mix it with the parsley (pinch off the stems). Stuff the fish with the mixture and a pat of butter. Hold the fish together with a toothpick. Turn the pieces in beaten egg and then in dried bread crumbs. Fry the fish in fat on a frying pan, 4-5 minutes on each side. Take the pieces from the pan and remove the toothpicks. Keep the fish warm. Add the rest of the butter to the pan and melt it together with a bit of vinegar. Serve the mixture as a sauce. This dish tastes excellent with small boiled potatoes and a green salad.

DANISH PORK OMELET
SERVES 4

This dish is so easy that one hardly needs a recipe! Anyone can make a Danish omelet, literally an egg cake - or can they? If the batter is too wet, is there too much milk, or should we blame the eggs? Lightly salted pork can be replaced by strips of ham or smoked pork. People often add flour to the batter to make it go further and to make it firmer, but I don't think it's necessary. A Danish omelet is probably more suitable for lunch than for dinner.

8-10 slices lightly salted lean pork
8 eggs
8 tbsp. milk

salt and pepper
a large bunch of chives

Beat the eggs with the milk. Fry the pork slices over medium heat until crispy and golden. Remove them from the pan. Pour in the egg batter and let it set. Add the pork to the pan just before the batter has completely set. Sprinkle with plenty of clipped chives. Season with salt and pepper. Serve immediately, right from the pan.

Hint: Tomato and cucumber slices can be arranged around the edge of the omelet.

ROOKS IN CREAM
SERVES 4

Rooks are spring game. This black, long-beaked bird, as large as a crow, can be shot from the first of May. It is not hard to spot a flock of rooks settling on someone's property - always in the highest tree. In the beginning of May, the young have taken flight, and can immediately risk being shot by a skilled hunter. In the country, roasted rooks were a common and cheap dish, and exceptionally delicious as well. Fish and game stores have rooks in season, from about the middle of May. Some people feel that rooks should be plucked, but I flay them with no bad conscience at all. Store-bought rooks are always flayed.

4-6 young rooks	3 dl heavy cream
salt and pepper	1 dl stock or bouillon
100 g smoked bacon	2-3 tbsp. finely grated dark rye
30 g butter	bread

Sprinkle the dressed rooks with salt and pepper. Cut the smoked bacon into small cubes and fry them until golden in a Dutch oven. Add the butter and heat until golden brown. Brown the rooks on all sides in the fat. Add half of the cream together with the bouillon. Simmer at medium heat for 30 minutes. Turn the birds frequently so they cook evenly. Remove them from the pot and add the rest of the cream together with the grated dark rye bread, to thicken the sauce and give it color. Boil for a moment and season to taste. Place the rooks on a deep platter and pour over the cream sauce. New potatoes and a salad are good accompaniments.

Hint: The rooks can be filled with parsley, like chickens. 1 dl heavy cream can be replaced by low-fat crème fraîche. Store-bought rooks do not have giblets; the liver can be very bitter.

OLD-FASHIONED BRAISED CHICKEN WITH CUCUMBER SALAD
SERVES 4

At Whitsuntide when I was a child, we had chicken stuffed with parsley and braised in a Dutch oven, since at this season young cocks were just the right size for the axe. The chickens were served with a good cream sauce and homemade cucumber salad. Today we often buy the supermarket's cheapest chicken on sale, but its taste and the structure of its meat have little to do with the fowl of the past. It is still possible to buy a freshly butchered country chicken worth the name.

2 fresh chickens, dressed	*Cucumber salad:*
3-4 bunches of parsley	I large cucumber
salt and pepper	2 dl table vinegar
75 g butter	a little water
3 dl heavy cream	2-3 tbsp. sugar (to taste)
(caramel color)	salt and pepper

Rinse the parsley well and remove the thickest stems. Sprinkle salt and pepper inside the cavity of the chickens. Fill with parsley and a big pat of butter. Close with skewers. Heat the butter in a Dutch oven until golden brown. Brown the chickens evenly on all sides. Lower the heat and add 1 dl of the cream. Cover and braise the chickens for 1 to 1 ¼ hours. Turn them frequently. It is important to cook the chickens until completely done. Remove the chickens and keep them warm. Add the rest of the cream and boil a few minutes. Season with salt and pepper. Cut the chickens into quarters and arrange them on a platter. Pour over a bit of the sauce and serve the rest separately.

Cucumber salad: Peel the cucumber if you like. Cut it into very thin slices. Dissolve the sugar in vinegar and add a little water if you do not want a strong marinade. Add the cucumber slices and season with salt and pepper.

Hint: The chicken giblets can be chopped finely and mixed with the parsley and butter as a stuffing or can be roasted in the pot and served with the chickens.

ROAST LAMB WITH PARSLEY
SERVES 6

Lamb is traditionally associated with Easter and spring. Freshly-butchered Danish lamb is naturally best, but it is early in the season and the Danish lambs are so small that there is not much taste to them yet. They are also very expensive and can be difficult to find. So I usually choose the excellent imported lambs which at this season come from New Zealand.

1 leg of lamb, saddle, or shoulder, c. 1 ½ kg	*Sauce:*
salt and pepper	c. 4 dl drippings
a bunch of parsley	1-2 tbsp. flour
(1 garlic clove)	(caramel color)
½ liter light bouillon (ready-made or from a cube)	salt and pepper

Cut deep little holes in the roast with a sharp knife. Fill them with parsley (and crushed garlic). Place the leg with the flat side up on a rack over a roasting pan, the saddle with the fatty side up. Criss-cross the fat with a knife. Rub the roast with salt and pepper.

Brown the roast for 15 minutes at 250°C. Lower the temperature to 160° and pour the bouillon into the pan. Turn the leg and roast it for c. 1 ½ hours - the saddle and shoulder for 1 to 1 ¼ hours.

Pour the drippings from the pan into a little saucepan; there should be about 4 dl. Skim off any excess fat. Bring the drippings to a boil and thicken to make a sauce. Season to taste.

Let the roast sit for 15-20 minutes before carving so that the juices spread evenly throughout the meat.

Accompaniment: Little boiled potatoes and cucumber salad. (See the recipe on p. 13.)

Hint: Mint sauce is also a good and traditional condiment for roast lamb. Remove the leaves from 4-5 fresh stems of mint. Cook the stems for 10 minutes in 1 ½ dl water, 2 tbsp. wine vinegar, and 1 tbsp. sugar. Sieve the liquid and add the finely chopped mint leaves. Let the sauce sit for a few hours and serve it hot or cold with roast lamb.

VEAL FRICASSEE
SERVES 4

This is a light dish, but with a motley mixture of vegetables it is certainly not boring. This wonderful spring and summer treat probably comes from French cuisine, where Fricassée de Veau is a classic.

1 ½ kg veal, shoulder or brisket	*Sauce:*
3 tsp. salt per liter water	3 tbsp. butter
3-4 carrots	3 tbsp. flour
5-6 leeks	½ liter stock
1 cauliflower	a bunch of parsley
250 g shelled peas	
bouquet garni of leek tops and parsley	

Put the meat in a pot and pour over enough water to just cover. Bring to a boil and skim the broth. Add the vegetables, except the cauliflower and peas. Add the bouquet garni. Remove the vegetables when they are tender. Simmer the meat until done, about 1 ½ hours in all. Dice the vegetables. Cut the cauliflower into small bouquets. Cook the cauliflower and peas last in a bit of the broth. Heat up the other vegetables in it as well. Melt the butter and cream it with the flour, then add the sieved broth gradually. Boil the mixture a few minutes and season with salt and pepper. Cut the meat into slices and arrange them on a hot platter. Top with the vegetables and pour over the sauce. Sprinkle with finely chopped parsley.

Hint: Little new potatoes can be added to the dish, which also tastes good with cooked asparagus pieces, white or green. Lamb fricassee is prepared the same way, but using a shorter cooking time for the meat.

ROAST SADDLE OF VENISON
SERVES 6

Saddle of venison is not just an autumn dish. Young bucks can be shot from May 16th to July 15th, but spring bucks are considered especially good by hunters.

1 saddle of venison, c. 3 kg	2 dl red wine
3 crushed juniper berries	2 dl bouillon
salt and pepper	2 dl cream
100 g butter	flour for thickening
½ kg little onions, shallots or	red currant or rowanberry jelly
mini-onions	

Cut the thickest sinews from the saddle; it is not necessary to cut all the thin sinews and sheaths off, since they can be removed during carving. Rub the saddle with crushed juniper berries, salt, and pepper. Cover the saddle with slices of butter. Brown the saddle on a roasting pan in a preheated 250°C oven for 10 minutes. Remove the pan from the oven and reduce the temperature to 150°. Add the peeled onions and any sinews and tendons to the pan. Mix half of the red wine, bouillon, and cream and pour it over the saddle. Return the pan to the oven and roast for a further 45-50 minutes. If you want the venison well done, keep it in for 10 more minutes. Remove the pan from the oven and transfer the meat to a platter, keeping it warm under foil. Pour the drippings through a sieve into a saucepan. Thin with the rest of the bouillon, cream, and red wine. Boil the sauce a few minutes and thicken it slightly. Season with jelly, salt, and pepper.

To serve: Carve the fillets from the saddle and cut them into diagonal slices. Turn the saddle and carve the tenderloin the same way. Serve the saddle with the slices elegantly back in place with the good venison sauce separately.

DANISH-STYLE FRENCH TOAST - "POOR KNIGHTS"
SERVES 4

Our parents' generation always made good use of old bread, and French toast was one of the desserts we remember with pleasure from our childhood. In Danish, the dish is called Poor Knights. Rich Knights probably appeared later, when it was possible to take a ferry over to Sweden and buy cheap almonds.

8 slices (dry) French bread   *Accompaniment:* Jam
1 ½ dl milk
8 tbsp. sugar
2 tsp. cinnamon
50 g butter

Let the bread slices soak up the milk for 10 minutes. Remove them and drain well. Mix the sugar and cinnamon and sprinkle it on the bread. Fry the slices in butter until light brown. Serve immediately with jam.
   "Rich Knights": After soaking the bread slices in milk, dip them in beaten egg and then in a mixture of 8 tbsp. sugar, 25 g finely chopped almonds, and 1 tsp. vanillin. Fry and serve as above.

RHUBARB PUDDING
SERVES 4

Rhubarb is one of the harbingers of spring. As early as April there are fresh shoots in the gardens and the delicate stalks can be found at the grocer's. Rhubarb contains oxalic acid, which binds calcium in the body. This acid can be neutralized by adding calcium chloride, available at grocery stores.

1 kg rhubarb   1 vanilla bean
¾ to 1 liter water   5 tbsp. potato flour
2 dl sugar   (slivered almonds)

Accompaniment: Milk or cream

Wash the rhubarb stalks and cut them into small pieces. Cook them in a saucepan with the water and split vanilla bean at medium heat for 15 minutes. Sieve the soup. If you use young, thin stalks there is no need to sieve the mixture. Return to the pan and add the sugar. Dissolve the potato flour in cold water. Bring the mixture to a boil. Remove from the heat and pour in the thickening all at one time, stirring constantly. Pour the pudding into a bowl and sprinkle with a bit of sugar to keep a skin from forming. Top with almond slivers. Let the pudding cool, but do not refrigerate, or the surface will loose its gloss. Serve with cream or milk.

RHUBARB COMPOTE
SERVES 6

½ kg tender rhubarb   175 g sugar
¼ liter water   1 vanilla bean

Rinse the rhubarb stalks and cut off the base and leaves. Cut the stalks into pieces 2 cm long. Cook a syrup from the water, sugar, and split vanilla bean. Add the rhubarb pieces and bring slowly to a boil. Remove the pot from the heat and let the mixture stand for 15 minutes. Discard the vanilla bean. Remove the rhubarb pieces carefully and put them in a serving bowl. Reduce the syrup slightly and pour it over the rhubarb.

Hint: Instead of making a syrup, put the rhubarb pieces in a baking dish and sprinkle them with sugar. Cover with foil if you like. The rhubarb will be tender after about 15 minutes at 150°C, or until it begins to get juicy.

SUMMER

(June - July - August)

This is summer in Denmark at its best, with plenty of wonderful berries. The first Danish strawberries come at around Midsummer, and soon there are red currants, raspberries, and black currants, just what is needed for our national dessert, Red Berry Soup, a kind of pudding with Cream, or perhaps for a portion of homemade jam for hot pancakes.

Young Danish cabbage is excellent creamed, and the Danish asparagus which is cut for Midsummer can now be bought in thick bunches for a reasonable price. There are firm, delicious potatoes from Samsø, since even though Denmark does import excellent potatoes from the Canary Islands and Italy, nothing tastes as good as a Danish new potato.

In the middle of July there are fresh peas, new carrots, cauliflower, and summer cabbage, and when the forest is greenest, the plaice is at its best, goes the Danish saying. When the summer's warm weather is at its peak from July into August, we eat fried eel with creamed potatoes. Eel is best late in the season and the catch is most plentiful after the full moon.

ASPARAGUS SOUP
SERVES 4

White or green asparagus can be used for the soup. Green asparagus does not have to be scraped and the cooking time is only half as long.

¼ kg fresh asparagus or a comparable amount canned
1 ¼ liter broth (or chicken bouillon from a cube)
20 g butter
3 tbsp. flour
2 egg yolks
(a little dry sherry or white wine)
salt and pepper

Danish pork omelet is served right from the pan with plenty of freshly clipped chives. See page 11.

Cut the stringy ends off the asparagus and scrape thinly from the tip towards the base, if you use the white variety. Just rinse green asparagus. Cut the stalks into pieces 3 cm long. Remove the tips and cook the rest in the broth for 8-10 minutes. Add the tips and cook them for 5 minutes. Remove the asparagus with a slotted spoon. Cream the softened butter and flour, whisk it into the soup and boil for 5 minutes. Beat the egg yolks together with a bit of the hot soup. Then pour it into the rest of the soup, beating constantly. The soup must not boil after the egg is added or it will curdle. Add the asparagus pieces and heat them. Season with salt, pepper, and sherry or white wine.

Hint: If you use canned asparagus, drain the stalks in a sieve. Mix the liquid in with the soup and add the asparagus pieces last. To make a richer soup, mix the egg yolks with a bit of heavy cream. Toasted croutons or little puff pastries can be served with the soup.

CAULIFLOWER SOUP
SERVES 4

The recipe can also be used for making broccoli and Brussels sprout soup.

1 large cauliflower	vegetable or
1 medium onion, chopped	chicken bouillon
2-3 finely diced celery stalks	from a cube)
2 finely diced carrots	1 to 1 ½ dl cream
2 tbsp. butter	salt and pepper
1 ¼ liter stock (or	a bunch of chives

Rinse the cauliflower and divide it into small bouquets. Braise the vegetables in butter in a saucepan. Add the cauliflower bouquets and the stock. Boil for 5 minutes. Remove the cauliflower bouquets and purée the rest in a blender or force through a sieve. Pour the mixture back into the saucepan and add the cream. Bring the soup to a boil and add the cauliflower bouquets. Season with salt and pepper. Sprinkle with clipped chives just before serving.

Hint: The soup can be thickened with two egg yolks just before the cauliflower bouquets are added, and you can also use a bit of crème fraîche together with the cream.

FRIED EEL WITH CREAMED POTATOES
SERVES 6

Choose eels that are not too big and fat. Medium-sized eels taste best.

2 ½ to 3 kg eels, gutted and skinned

For breading:	*Creamed potatoes:*
1 egg	2 kg potatoes
1 dl sifted dry bread crumbs	3 tbsp. butter
salt and pepper	3 tbsp. flour
75-100 g butter	c. ½ liter milk and cream
a couple of lemons	salt and pepper
	a bunch of chives

Rinse the eels and dry them thoroughly. Cut them into pieces 5 cm long and turn them first in the beaten egg, then in the bread crumbs. Season with salt and pepper. Fry them in butter for 10-15 minutes. Make sure that the pieces fry evenly on all sides until crisp.
   Creamed potatoes: Peel and boil the potatoes in lightly salted water. Dice the potatoes. Melt the butter and cream it with the flour. Dilute with milk and cream. Boil the mixture for a few minutes before adding the diced potatoes. Season with salt and pepper. Sprinkle with plenty of clipped chives just before serving. Serve the melted butter from the pan with the eels and garnish with lemon wedges.

EEL RAGOUT
SERVES 4

This is an old Danish dish. You can use small eels, which are less expensive.

1 kg small fresh (skinned) eels	2 sprigs of thyme
3 onions	6 whole peppercorns
3 tart apples	3 dl water
½ kg potatoes	salt
50 g butter	

Cut the eels into pieces 5-6 cm long. Skin and slice the onions and cut the apples into thin wedges. Peel and slice the potatoes. Arrange the eel, onion, apples, and potatoes in layers in a greased Dutch oven. Add the thyme, whole peppercorns, and salt, and dot with pats of butter. Pour in the water. Cover and simmer for 30 to 45 minutes. Serve with vinegar and hearty bread.

FISH BALLS
SERVES 4

Good fish mousseline can be bought from most Danish fish dealers, but the homemade variety is still always best. Coalfish and cod are suitable for fish mousseline if you do not do any fishing yourself and can get freshly caught pike, which is also excellent for the purpose.

½ kg fillet of cod or coalfish	1 dl milk
1 little skinned onion	1 dl heavy cream
2 tbsp. potato flour	1 tsp. salt
2 tbsp. flour	a dash of white pepper
3 egg whites	fat for frying

Cut the fish into small pieces and put it through a meat grinder together with the quartered onion. Mix the potato flour and flour with the fish and add the egg whites. Stir in the milk and cream a little at a time. Season with salt and pepper.

Melt the fat in a frying pan, then remove it from the heat while you shape the fish balls and arrange them on the pan. Fry over very low heat and make sure that they do not get crusty too quickly, or they will deflate into cakes.

Serve with lemon wedges, boiled potatoes, and lemon sauce.

Lemon Sauce: Melt 3 tbsp. butter in a saucepan and cream with 2 tbsp. flour. Gradually add 4 dl light bouillon, broth, or water. Boil for a few minutes. Add 2-3 tbsp. lemon juice. Whisk 2 egg yolks into 1 dl cream. Beat into the sauce and heat well, but do not let it boil or it will curdle. Season to taste with salt and pepper.

Veal fricassee with vegetables in season. See page 14.

FRIED PLAICE
SERVES 4

In the summer, when the forest is greenest, the plaice is at its best. It can be fried à la Meunière, sautéed in butter, or breaded. Plaice is usually skinned on one side before frying, but try to fry plaice unskinned. The fish will keep its flavor and juiciness and the skin will be crispy.

4 fresh plaice	1 dl dried bread crumbs
2-3 tbsp. flour	salt and pepper
salt and pepper	fat for frying
or 1 egg	1 lemon

Gut and rinse the plaice and dredge them in a mixture of flour, salt, and pepper or in egg and dried bread crumbs seasoned with salt and pepper. If you use flour, brown the plaice very quickly on both sides before you finish frying them or the flour will get sticky. If you use bread crumbs, the fish should be fried completely on one side before turning and frying it on the other.

Serve the plaice with lemon wedges, the butter from the pan, and little new potatoes. Parsley sauce (see p. 37) is a wonderful accompaniment, or you can use lemon or Hollandaise sauce. A good accompaniment in the summer is cucumbers with cream.

Cucumbers with cream:
Cut a large cucumber into sticks 5 cm long and ½ cm thick. Sprinkle them with salt and let them stand for half an hour. Rinse and dry. Put them in a saucepan with (heavy) cream and cook them until tender, 3-4 minutes. Mix in chopped parsley or clipped chives and season with salt and pepper.

SALTED BRISKET OF BEEF WITH CREAMED SPRING CABBAGE
SERVES 4

This dish is especially good when the cabbage is firm and juicy. Your butcher will be glad to salt the brisket for you.

a brisket of beef (lightly salted), c. 2 kg	2 dl cabbage cooking water
1 spring cabbage	2-3 dl milk or cream
3 tbsp. butter	salt and white pepper
3 tbsp. flour	a little ground nutmeg

Cover the brisket with water and cook until tender, about 2 hours. Divide the cabbage into 4-5 wedges and cook them in lightly salted water for 15 minutes. Melt the butter and cream it with the flour. Dilute with the liquid from the cabbage and with milk or cream. Boil the sauce and season with salt, pepper, and ground nutmeg. Chop the cabbage finely and mix it into the liquid, or arrange whole pieces of cabbage on a deep platter and pour the sauce over them. Carve the brisket and serve with the creamed spring cabbage.

BRAISED SQUAB
SERVES 4

Only braise young pigeons - squabs - since old ones cannot be cooked until tender. Since it is hard to see a pigeon's age, you'll have to trust your fish and game dealer. Allow at least 1 squab person, and 1 ½ or 2 if your guests have a good appetite.

4-6 squabs	*Sauce:*
salt and pepper	drippings
6-8 thin slices of fresh pork fat	2 dl heavy cream
50 g butter	red or black currant jelly
½ dl bouillon	flour for thickening
½ dl heavy cream	

Sprinkle the dressed squabs inside and out with salt and pepper. Bard them with thin slices of pork fat and brown them on all sides in butter in a Dutch oven. Reduce the heat and add the bouillon and heavy cream. Cover and simmer for 30-40 minutes. Turn them frequently to ensure that they cook evenly.

When the squabs are tender, remove them from the Dutch oven and add the cream. Boil and thicken. Season with currant jelly, salt, and pepper. Halve the squabs and arrange them on a heated platter. Pour over a bit of the sauce and serve the rest separately.

Serve with little boiled potatoes, turned in chopped parsley, and salad.

Hint: Squabs taste good stuffed with a few fresh sage leaves. You can add little fried button mushrooms to the sauce or serve them on the side.

MEATBALLS
SERVES 4

No meatballs ever taste as good as mother made them, and there is no doubt that meatballs are the Danes' national dish. No Danish food can be prepared and served in so many different ways. The meatballs from North Schleswig, which use dried bread crumbs or bread instead of flour, are justifiably famous. We find meatballs abroad, too: Spanish, French, Italian, Greek, Mexican, and many other types, so the meatball is widely traveled. Where it originally came from nobody knows.

½ kg ground pork
(or half pork, half beef)
4-5 tbsp. flour
1 egg or 2 egg whites
1 medium grated onion
2-3 dl milk, soda water,
or stock (bouillon)
salt and pepper
fat for frying

Creamed cabbage:
1 head of white cabbage
2 dl heavy cream
salt, pepper, and ground nutmeg

Combine the ground meat with the flour and egg (egg whites) and mix in the grated onion. Add the liquid a little at a time, blending well. Mix

"Mother's" meatballs are served with boiled potatoes and salad or creamed cabbage.

in the salt and pepper. Let the mixture stand for half an hour to see if it can take more liquid. Heat the fat on a pan until golden and drop the meatballs on with a soup spoon. It is important to have the fat hot enough before putting on the meatballs or they will stick to the pan. Then reduce the heat and fry the meatballs until done.

Creamed white cabbage: Chop the cabbage finely and boil it in lightly salted water for 10 minutes. Drain well and put it in a pot with heavy cream. Season with salt, pepper, and ground nutmeg. Simmer for 10 minutes, covered, and then for 5-10 minutes, uncovered. Stir frequently to keep the cabbage from sticking.

Hint: You can add chopped herbs to the meatballs - parsley, dill, and chives - and you can also substitute smoked ham for a bit of the pork/beef.

Dead Meatballs are made of cooked, ground meat mixed with grated onion, ground smoked pork, egg, and dried bread crumbs.

Giant Meatballs: Heat the fat until golden in a pan and cover it with all the meat mixture. Fry the meatball completely on one side first before you turn it (using a lid) and fry the other side. Sprinkle with chopped parsley, sliced tomatoes, green peppers, etc.

BOILED SALTED, SMOKED SADDLE OF PORK
SERVES 6

Choose a saddle of pork that has been cured with a 3-4% saline solution.

1 kg salted, smoked saddle of pork	*Accompaniment:*
	1 kg fresh spinach
1 onion	4-5 tbsp. butter
	salt and pepper

Put the meat in a pot and pour over enough water to cover. Add the quartered, skinned onion.

Cover and simmer the meat for 30 minutes. Turn off the heat and let the meat stand for 20 minutes in its broth. Remove the smoked skin before carving the meat.

Accompaniment: Rinse the spinach well in several changes of cold water. Melt the butter in a saucepan and add the spinach. Steam the spinach briefly so that it just collapses. Sprinkle with salt and pepper and serve with boiled saddle of pork accompanied by little boiled potatoes.

Hint: You can also serve boiled vegetables in season together with creamed or melted butter. Red wine or mushroom sauce also makes a fine accompaniment.

Glazed saddle of pork: Remove the smoked skin after cooking and place the saddle on a baking dish. Brush the meat with mustard and sprinkle with sugar. Dot with pats of butter and glaze at 250°C for 10-20 minutes.

FRIED PORK CHOPS
SERVES 4

A delicious, juicy fried pork chop requires good meat and gentle frying. Our grandmothers breaded the chops before they were put on the pan, and many cooks still think this is the best way, especially when they mix grated cheese with the bread crumbs.

4 thick pork chops   salt and pepper
(breading: 1 egg and   fat for frying
1 dl dried bread crumbs)

Accompaniment: Vegetables in season

Pound the chops with the heel of your hand. Clip the edges all around so they do not curl during frying.

Breading: Turn the chops in beaten egg and then in dried bread crumbs (mixed with grated cheese).

Season the chops with salt and freshly ground pepper.

If the chops are not breaded, set them on a hot frying pan, fatty edges down. Fry the fat until golden.

Add fat to the pan and heat it until light brown. Brown the chops on both sides. Reduce the heat and fry for 4-6 minutes on each side.

Arrange the chops on a hot platter and garnish with boiled vegetables.

Hint: The chops can be seasoned with paprika, curry powder, rosemary, oregano, or other spices and herbs. A green salad with boiled sliced potatoes makes a good accompaniment to chops in the summer.

RED BERRY SOUP WITH CREAM
SERVES 4

This is the summer's best dessert, and as far as I know, it is made only in Denmark. Red berry soup can be made with whole berries, with the liquid left after the berries are sieved, or with half of each. I prefer half and half, keeping the berries' flavor and consistency. People usually make red berry soup from red currants, black currants, and raspberries. I usually add strawberries, too.

300 g rhubarb stalks
4 dl water
250 g red currants
200 g black currants
250 g fresh strawberries

350 g fresh raspberries
c. 150 g sugar, or to taste
potato flour or cornstarch for thickening

Cut the rhubarb stalks into little pieces and put them in a pot with the water, red currants, and half of the black currants. Simmer gently for 5-6 minutes. Sieve the mixture. Return it to the pot and add the rest of the black currants together with the strawberries and sugar. Cook briefly before adding the raspberries. Bring to a boil and stir. Dissolve the starch in a bit of cold water and mix it into the boiling-hot pudding. Pour into a serving bowl and sprinkle with a little sugar to keep a skin from forming. Serve with cream.

Hint: You can sprinkle on finely chopped almonds before serving. Cherries can be added to the other sieved berries.

Red berry soup is the summer's best dessert.

BUTTERMILK DESSERT
SERVES 4

When it begins to get warm, this is one of the most popular desserts for everyday meals. It's best when made with old-fashioned buttermilk.

2 egg yolks
c. 1 dl sugar, or to taste
1 tbsp. grated lemon peel

1 ¼ liter buttermilk
whipped cream

Whisk the egg yolks with the sugar and stir in the buttermilk and grated lemon peel. Refrigerate before serving. Top with mounds of whipped cream or serve whipped cream on the side together with rusks.

Hint: You can add vanilla or mix in sliced bananas, pieces of orange, or fresh berries, depending on the time of year.

Medley: Add 1 dl grated dark rye bread and 50 g raisins. You can also add chopped almonds.

ICE CREAM
SERVES 6

Before the freezer appeared in nearly every Danish home, ice cream was made in a bucket placed in a mixture of ice and salt. The bucket had to be turned constantly so that the ice cream froze evenly, without any ice crystals forming. This method was common just 30 years ago, when life was not as easy as it is today: the ice cream mixture can now be put directly into your freezer.

½ liter light cream
1 vanilla bean

4 egg yolks
60 g sugar

Bring the cream to a boil with the split vanilla bean. Whisk together the egg yolks and sugar. Pour the boiling-hot cream into the mixture, beating constantly. Discard the vanilla bean. Return to the saucepan and bring the mixture nearly to a boil (in a double boiler), beating constantly. The crème must not boil or it will curdle. Cool the crème and add flavoring (chocolate pieces, sugared berries, nougat, etc.) before freezing.

CONSTITUTION DAY DESSERT
SERVES 4

This classical dessert in red and white - the colors of the Danish flag - was traditionally served in many homes on June 5th, Constitution Day. The dessert is just as good and popular today.

¾ kg tender rhubarb	4 dl light cream
125 g sugar	1 vanilla bean
Crème:	4 gelatin leaves
4 eggs (separated)	1 ½ dl heavy cream
4 tbsp. sugar	slivered or flaked almonds

Cut the rhubarb into pieces 2-cm long and put them in a baking dish. Sprinkle with sugar. Bake at 160°C for 25 minutes. The rhubarb should not turn mushy.

Bring the cream to a boil with the split vanilla bean. Soak the gelatin leaves in cold water. (To use powdered gelatin, see the conversion table on p. 4). Whisk the egg yolks and the sugar and add the boiling-hot cream. Discard the vanilla bean. Shake any excess water off the gelatin leaves and stir them into the liquid; the gelatin will melt immediately. Cool the crème, but stir occasionally to prevent a skin from forming. Beat the egg whites until stiff and fold them into the crème before it stiffens completely. Put the cold rhubarb mixture in a bowl and top with the crème, while still slightly soft. Garnish with whipped cream and sprinkle with slivered or flaked almonds.

SUGARED CURRANTS
SERVES 4

This is a real summer delicacy. White and yellow currants are not as tart as the red ones.

½ kg fresh red, white, or yellow currants
200 g sugar

Rinse the currants in cold water and remove any stems. Drain well and place in a bowl, alternating with layers of sugar. Shake the berries so that the sugar is evenly distributed but the berries remain whole. Refrigerate for a hour before eating. Serve plain or with whipped cream.

PANCAKES
SERVES 4

Pancakes are eaten the year round, but they taste best of all served fresh from the pan, rolled around a portion of lightly sugared summer berries, for example strawberries, raspberries, or blueberries.

200 g flour	3 eggs
1 tsp. sugar	4 dl milk
¼ tsp. salt	3 tbsp. beer
a bit of grated lemon peel	fat for frying

Combine the flour, sugar, salt, and grated lemon peel. Beat the eggs and mix them into the flour with a bit of milk. Whisk in the rest of the milk together with the beer, and beat until smooth. Fry thin pancakes in the golden-brown fat.

CITY HALL PANCAKES

According to reliable sources, City Hall Pancakes should be made this way:
Make thin pancakes as above. Fill them with liqueur crème.

Crème:	
3 gelatin leaves	2 tbsp. liqueur
3 egg yolks	50 g almonds
3 tbsp. powdered sugar	25 g candied orange peel
	2 ½ dl heavy cream

Soak the gelatin leaves in water for 5 minutes. (To use powdered gelatin, see the conversion table on p. 4.) Beat the egg yolks and sugar well and stir in the liqueur. Blanch and chop the almonds. Whip the cream until stiff. Shake all the water from the gelatin leaves and melt them in a double boiler. Pour the melted gelatin in a thin stream into the egg mixture, beating the whole time. Stir in the chopped almonds and candied peel and carefully fold in the whipped cream. Roll the pancakes around the crème and sprinkle with powdered sugar.

Pancakes are served the year round as dessert, and they taste wonderful hot from the pan with jam.

AUTUMN

(September-October-November)

In the old days, September was called the fish month, and with good reason, because at this time of year there is plenty of good fish, perhaps first and foremost good autumn herring. Autumn is also hunting time, when we can see newly shot pheasants hanging in their fine plumage outside the fish and game dealers . The grocer has good Danish apples, fresh hazel nuts, and elderberries and rose hips for making fruit pudding and juice concentrate. There are fine leeks and celeriac, and in the autumn we find large bunches of juicy parsley to sprinkle on Burning Love or to add to the milk sauce for fried herring. For mushroom enthusiasts and experts, the autumn months are the best time of all, but there is now a good selection of various mushrooms to be found at the grocer's - so at least you can be completely certain that they are edible.

TARTLETS WITH CREAMED FISH
MAKES 12-15 TARTLETS

Tartlets with creamed fish or chicken, accompanied by sweet sauterne, was a typical first course for a fine dinner. Tartlets are still popular, but unlike in the old days, they can now be bought at the supermarket. Home-baked tartlets naturally taste much better, especially if they are served with a good filling.

250 g flour
150 g butter
a pinch of salt
1 egg
1 tbsp. cream or water

Filling:
200 g shelled shrimp
1 500 g can asparagus pieces
2 dl asparagus liquid
1 ½ dl cream
3 tbsp. butter
2 tbsp. flour
salt and pepper
dill

Cut the butter into the flour and mix in the salt. Add the egg and cream or water and knead. Refrigerate for half an hour. Roll the dough thinly and cut out little circles large enough to cover the outside of a tartlet mold. Press the dough around the ungreased molds and prick with a fork. Place the molds upside down on a baking sheet and bake for c. 10 minutes at 225°C.

Filling: Bring the cream and asparagus liquid to a boil. Cream the butter and flour and beat the mixture into the liquid. Boil for a few minutes. Warm the shrimp and asparagus pieces in the sauce.
Fill the warm tartlets and garnish with dill sprigs.

FRIED HERRING WITH PARSLEY SAUCE
SERVES 4

Herring is still one of our cheapest ingredients, and one might wonder why people do not eat more of it. It can hardly be the bones, which a fish dealer can easily remove. Plump Danish autumn herrings dredged in rye flour, fried, and served with parsley sauce is one of the best herring dishes. If the herring has roe, let it remain in the fish during frying, or take it out and fry briefly on the same pan. You might fry a double portion while you're at it and put half in a vinegar marinade.

1 to 1 ½ kg fresh herring	*Parsley sauce:*
1 ½ to 2 dl rye flour	3 tbsp, butter
salt and pepper	2 tbsp. flour
c. 75 g butter for frying	3 dl milk
lemon	a bunch of parsley
	salt and pepper

Gut and rinse the herring. Slash each herring a couple of times across the back so that the skin does not pull together during frying.

Dredge the herrings in a mixture of rye flour and salt and pepper. Heat the butter until golden and fry the herrings for 4-5 minutes, depending on the thickness.

Parsley Sauce: Melt the butter in a saucepan and stir in the flour. Dilute with boiling-hot milk. Boil for a few minutes before adding the freshly chopped parsley. Season to taste with salt and pepper.

Arrange the hot herring on a serving platter and garnish with lemon wedges. Serve with little boiled potatoes and (dill) vinegar.

Fried Herring in Vinegar: Boil a marinade of 2 dl vinegar, ½ dl water, 6-8 tbsp. sugar (to taste), 2 bay leaves, a sprig of thyme, and 6 coarsely crushed peppercorns. Cool the marinade before pouring it over the warm herrings. Refrigerate until the next day. Garnish with plenty of raw onion rings.

BOILED COD WITH ALL THE FIXINGS
SERVES 4

Cod is best in the autumn and winter months, so the old rule that it is at its finest in months with the letter "r" - in both Danish and English - is not far off the mark.

1 cod (over 2 kg, or one large piece)	4-5 whole peppercorns
Stock per liter of water:	2 bay leaves
1 tbsp. salt	

Accompaniments:
100 g butter
special fish mustard, chopped hard-boiled eggs and/or capers, grated horseradish

Scale and rinse the cod and remember to remove the black membrane inside and the white bladder.

Put the fish in a pot (on a rack). Pour over enough water to just cover the fish. Add the salt, peppercorns, and bay leaves. Bring the fish slowly to a boil. Skim the stock and simmer the fish gently for 15-20 minutes. The water should just bubble at the edges. Remove the fish with a slotted spoon and place it on a heated platter.

Serve with butter, special fish mustard, chopped hard-boiled eggs, and boiled (mealy) potatoes.

Hint: Instead of melted butter, dilute the fish mustard with a bit of the stock and serve it as a sauce.

If the cod is too large to fit into a pot, it can be steamed in the oven. Place the cod in a greased baking pan. Sprinkle inside and out with coarse salt. Pour on a bit of water and cover with aluminum foil. Steam at 200°C for 40 minutes.

Boiled cod is served with chopped hard-boiled egg,
special fish mustard, boiled potatoes, and butter sauce.

"BURNING LOVE"
SERVES 4

I have always had a weakness for this simple dish, which was always on the dinner table when it was washing day. It can be made into "Green Love" by adding finely chopped steamed leeks and chopped parsley.

1 ½ kg potatoes	salt and white pepper
c. 3 dl milk (or half	1 kg lightly salted lean pork
milk and half cream)	3 medium onions
30-50 g butter	a bunch of parsley

Peel the potatoes and boil them in unsalted water. Cut the pork into small cubes and fry until golden and crispy. Peel and slice the onions. Fry them on the same pan in the remaining fat.

Mash the potatoes and beat in the milk and butter until fluffy. Season to taste with salt and pepper.

Heap the mashed potatoes on a hot serving platter and top with the pork cubes and onion. Sprinkle with chopped parsley before serving.

Hint: The dish can be made more hearty by adding 125 g fried cocktail sausages, and you can also add fried button mushrooms and finely diced green or red pepper.

STEWED CHICKEN IN ASPARAGUS SAUCE
SERVES 6

Buy a good stewing hen or a meaty pullet from your butcher.

1 large tender hen or pullet, dressed	*Asparagus Sauce:*
c. 2 liters water	6 dl chicken soup
1 tbsp. salt	1 can white asparagus
2 carrots	3 tbsp. butter
1 onion	3 tbsp. flour
1-2 leeks	2 egg yolks
1 Hamburg parsley root	1 dl cream
bouquet garni of leek tops	salt and pepper
and a bunch of parsley	

Put the hen in a pot, adding enough water to cover, about 2 liters. Bring to a boil and skim the surface. Add the salt, vegetables, cut into large pieces, and the bouquet garni. Cover and simmer until tender, about 1½ hours. Remove the hen and keep it warm under foil. Sieve the broth.

Sauce: Put 6 dl of the sieved broth in a saucepan. Add the liquid from the can of asparagus. Bring to a boil. Cream the butter and flour and whisk into the broth. Boil the sauce for a few minutes. Beat the egg yolks and cream. Whisk the mixture into the sauce. Bring the sauce almost to a boil, but do not boil or it will curdle. Add the pieces of asparagus and season to taste.

Cut the hen into serving pieces and arrange it on a hot platter. Pour on a little asparagus sauce and serve the rest separately.

Serve with little puff pastries or small boiled potatoes.

Hint: Instead of asparagus sauce, you can use button mushrooms. Saute ½ kg sliced button mushrooms in a little butter before adding to the sauce, prepared the same way as for asparagus sauce.

MEAT PATTIES WITH ONIONS
SERVES 4

Whether you want crisp or soft fried onions with your meat patties is a matter of taste. Soft onions must be fried in plenty of fat. You can also add 1 tbsp. of water to the pan just before removing the onions.

600 g ground beef	2 dl bouillon
salt and pepper	(a little cream)
50 butter or margarine	flour for thickening
3 onions	

Form the meat into 4 large or 6 medium-sized patties. Season with salt and pepper. Peel and slice the onions. Brown half of the fat on a pan and fry the onions in it. Set aside.

Add the rest of the fat to the pan and heat until golden. Brown the patties on both sides, lower the temperature, and fry until done, about 3 minutes on each side. Remove the patties from the pan and add the bouillon and a little cream. Bring to a boil and thicken into a sauce. Arrange the onion rings on top of the patties and serve with boiled potatoes and cucumber salad. Serve the sauce separately.

MEAT LOAF
SERVES 6

This kind of meat loaf - known in Danish as mock hare - is a roll of ground beef topped with bacon slices. According to older recipes a thick brown sauce should be poured over the hare as it roasts. I have left out the sauce here since the meat tastes just as good without it.

1 kg ground beef
c. 1 dl sifted dried bread crumbs
1 egg
1 dl bouillon or milk
1 little grated onion
1 tsp. ground ginger
salt and pepper
c. 8 thin slices of bacon
½ liter bouillon
2 dl light cream

Sauce:
pan juices
1 dl cream
flour for thickening
red currant or rowanberry jelly

Mix the ground beef with the bread crumbs, and stir in the egg. Add the grated onion. Mix 1 dl of bouillon or milk into the meat a little at a time, blending well. Season with ginger, salt, and pepper.

Shape the meat into an oblong loaf and put it in a greased baking dish or little baking pan. Cover with the bacon slices.

Brown the loaf at 250°C for 15 minutes. Reduce the temperature to 160° and pour the boiling bouillon and cream mixture over the meat. Roast for another 40 minutes.

Pour the drippings into a little saucepan and dilute with cream. Bring to a boil and thicken into a sauce. Season to taste with jelly, salt, and pepper. If the sauce is too pale, add caramel color. Serve with glazed potatoes and a salad.

Hint: Instead of the traditional types of potato, you can make baked potatoes Hasselbacken style. Allow 1 medium-large potato per person. Peel the potatoes and cut deep, thin slices in each, but do not cut all the way through. Put the potatoes into a greased baking dish. Brush with melted butter or oil and sprinkle with salt and pepper. Bake the potatoes in the oven after you have browned the meat loaf.

Grandmother's apple cake should be garnished with whipped cream and jelly. See page 50.

BROWN CABBAGE WITH PORK
SERVES 4

This is a hearty winter dish that warms and is suitably filling. Instead of lean pork you can use a meaty collarbone.

1 medium-sized head of cabbage	salt, pepper, and thyme
3-4 tbsp. sugar or syrup	¾ to 1 kg lightly salted lean pork
30 g butter	2-3 dl water

Discard the outermost leaves and slice the cabbage thinly. Brown the sugar in a thick-bottomed pot and add the fat. Turn the sliced cabbage in the mixture. Season with salt, pepper, and thyme.

Add the pork and the water. Cover and simmer for an hour.

Slice the pork and serve it with the cabbage together with homemade bread and mustard.

Hint: You can add 4-6 luncheon sausages for the last 5 minutes of the cooking time. Serve the sausages together with the pork.

PORK RIB ROAST
SERVES 4

To make sure you get crispy crackling, I suggest you boil the fatty side for 20 minutes before roasting. It can easily be done with such a little roast.

1 pork rib roast, c. 1 kg	*Potatoes au gratin:*
2-3 bay leaves	1 kg potatoes
salt and pepper	salt and pepper
2-3 medium onions	a bunch of parsley
2 sprigs of thyme	3-4 dl cream
½ liter water or bouillon	(or half cream, half milk)

Make sure to cut deep slashes in the fatty side. Boil the fatty side in water on a frying pan for 20 minutes. Turn the roast and put it in a baking dish or little baking pan. Season with salt and pepper and stick the bay leaves into the slashes in the fat.

Brown at 250°C for 15 minutes. Reduce the temperature to 175° and arrange the quartered onions and thyme around the roast. Pour over the liquid. Put the potatoes au gratin in the oven at the same time.

Potatoes au gratin: Peel and slice the potatoes and arrange them in a greased baking dish. Season with salt and pepper and sprinkle on chopped parsley. Add the cream.

Roast both the meat and the potatoes for about 1 hour. Pour the drippings into a little saucepan and thicken into a sauce. Season to taste.

Hint: Instead of potatoes au gratin, you can serve home fried or baked potatoes. Red cabbage and glazed potatoes are also popular accompaniments to rib roast.

ROAST PHEASANT IN CREAM SAUCE
SERVES 8

If you buy pheasants from a fish and game dealer, it costs a bit extra to have the birds plucked, but it is worth it. The old-fashioned roasting method is to bard the birds with thin slices of fresh pork fat before browning them in a pot. Although you can still use this method, I have not done it here.

4 young pheasants, each 600-800 g
salt and pepper
50 g butter
3 dl bouillon (stock

or chicken bouillon cube)
2 ½ dl heavy cream
thickening
red currant or rowanberry jelly

Rub salt and pepper into the dressed pheasants. If you use pork slices, cover breast and drumstick. Tie with cotton twine. Brown on all sides in butter in a Dutch oven. Reduce the heat and add half of the bouillon and half of the cream.

Cover and simmer the pheasants for 45-50 minutes. Remove from the pot and keep warm under foil.

Add the rest of the bouillon and cream. Bring to a boil and thicken into a sauce. Season with jelly, salt, and pepper.

Serve with little boiled potatoes and Waldorf salad. (See the recipe for Roast Wild Duck, p. 46.)

Hint: The pheasants can be stuffed with pitted green grapes, and you can substitute red wine for half of the bouillon. Instead of thickening with flour, you can cream 4 tbsp. butter and 4 tbsp. flour and whisk the mixture into the sauce to make it more robust.

ROAST WILD DUCK
SERVES 6

It is a tradition to bard both wild birds and game with pork fat, fresh or smoked. Our grandmothers always did it. I think it should only be done for a few birds with dry meat. If wild ducks are plucked, browned gently, and roasted at a low temperature, I think barding is unnecessary. If you want the smoked taste imparted by smoked pork fat, you can brown a few cubes of pork fat with the other fat you use.

3 young wild ducks, dressed	50 g butter
salt and pepper	3 dl bouillon
5-6 crushed juniper berries	3 dl heavy cream
(a couple of slices of smoked	red currant or rowanberry jelly
bacon)	

Rub the ducks inside and out with salt, pepper, and crushed juniper berries. If you use it, cut the smoked pork fat into little cubes.

Fry the fat cubes in a Dutch oven and add the butter. Heat until golden. Brown the ducks on all sides. Reduce the heat and add half of the bouillon and half of the cream. Cover and simmer for about 1 hour. Turn the birds often and baste with the rest of the cream. When they are tender, remove them from the pot and keep them warm under foil.

Sieve the juices and return them to the pot. Add the rest of the bouillon and bring it to a boil. Thicken into a sauce and season with jelly, salt, and pepper.

Serve with boiled potatoes and the good sauce. Waldorf Salad is excellent on the side.

Waldorf Salad: Cut 2-3 robust apples into cubes and mix with 2-3 finely chopped celery stalks, a bunch of grapes, and 50 g coarsely chopped walnuts. Fold in a dressing made with 2 dl crème fraîche and 1 dl cream.

Roast duck filled with prunes and apples is a traditional Danish Christmas dish. Duck is served with glazed potatoes, red cabbage, and pickled cucumbers. See page 61, 62, 13.

ELDERBERRY SOUP WITH APPLES
SERVES 4

Elderberries contain more iron than any other Danish fruit. Danes know that elderberries help ease colds, sore throats, and other ailments. Good elderberry soup has to be so strong that the pieces of apple are dyed purple. Old-fashioned Danish elderberry soup was always served with dumplings.

1 kg ripe elderberries	*Dumplings:*
1 liter water	40 g flour
1 lemon	40 g potato flour
2-3 robust apples	1 ½ dl water
c. 125 g sugar	50 g butter
potato flour	2 eggs
	½ tsp. salt
	1 tsp. sugar

Cut off the thickest stems. Cook the berries in water for 5-6 minutes. Sieve the liquid. Peel the apples and cut them into wedges. Slice the lemon thinly. Return the soup to the pot and add the sugar, lemon, and apples.

Boil for 5 minutes and thicken slightly.

Dumplings: Blend the flour, potato flour, and water until smooth and bring to a boil. Add the butter and boil, stirring constantly. Remove from the stove and cool slightly.

Stir in the eggs and add the salt and sugar. Use a pastry tube without a nozzle or teaspoon to form little dumplings, and put them direct in boiling, lightly salted water. Simmer (do not boil) for 3-4 minutes.

Remove the dumplings with a slotted spoon and dip them in cold water before draining them in a bowl. Add the dumplings to the soup just before serving.

Hint: If you like the taste, boil a piece of cinnamon bark with the soup.

ROSE HIP SOUP
SERVES 4

Rose hips are rich in vitamin C, which is why they are called the oranges of the north. You can use rose hips to make jam, juice concentrate, purée, sauce, etc. Your main ingredient is free since the dog rose grows wild in many places.

¾ kg rose hips
1 ½ liters water
c. 100 g sugar

lemon juice
potato flour

Accompaniment: Whipped cream

Cut the flower and stem from the rose hip, cut it in two and scrape out the seeds (done most easily with a teaspoon). Put the fruit in a pot with the water and bring to a boil. Boil until tender for about half an hour. Purée the fruit through a sieve. Bring the purée to a boil with the sugar and add a little lemon juice. Thicken with potato flour dissolved in cold water.
　　Serve piping hot with whipped cream. Rusks can be served on the side.

APPLESAUCE
SERVES 4

Juicy cooking apples are best for applesauce. If you use a type of apple that remains firm, you can use a little potato flour diluted with water to thicken the sauce.

1 ½ kg cooking apples
c. 1 dl water

c. 200 g sugar
1 vanilla bean

Accompaniment: Milk or cream

Peel and core the apples. Cut them into pieces. Put the apple, split vanilla bean, and water in a saucepan. Cover and simmer. Discard the vanilla bean and add the sugar. Pour the applesauce into a serving bowl and chill. Serve with cold milk or cream.
　　Hints: Applesauce can be used for other desserts, for example

Apples with Rice: Fold 2 dl whipped cream into 2 dl cooked long-grained rice. Alternate layers of the rice mixture and applesauce in a bowl. Garnish with whipped cream and dabs of red currant jelly.

APPLE CAKE
SERVES 4

Robust, aromatic cooking apples are used in old-fashioned apple cake.

1 kg (cooking) apples	*Dried bread-crumb mixture:*
80 g sugar	1 dl sugar
a little water	200 g dried bread crumbs
1 vanilla bean	75 g butter or margarine
	4 large or 8 small macaroons

To garnish: Whipped cream and jelly

Peel, slice, and boil the apples with the split vanilla bean and a little water. When the apples are completely soft, remove the pot from the heat, discard the vanilla bean, and stir in the sugar. Cool the applesauce. Mix the sugar and dried bread crumbs. Heat the fat on a pan until golden and add the bread-crumb mixture. Toast until crisp and golden. Remove from the heat and add the crushed macaroons. Arrange alternating layers of applesauce and the dried bread-crumb mixture in a bowl, beginning and ending with the mixture. Top with whipped cream and garnish with dabs of jelly.

Baked apple cake: Arrange alternating layers of applesauce and the mixture in a greased baking dish. End with the mixture and top with dabs of butter. Bake at 200°C for 20 minutes. Serve warm with cold whipped cream.

Quick apple cake: Alternate layers of the dried bread-crumb mixture with coarsely grated apples mixed with a little sugar. Top with whipped cream and garnish with coarsely chopped nuts.

Apple cake from Funen: Use 100 g dried bread crumbs and leave out the macaroons, using 150 g grated dark rye bread instead. Bake as above.

LEMON MOUSSE
SERVES 4

This was a Sunday dessert, and for special occasions such as confirmations and silver wedding anniversaries sherry or rum was used as the flavoring.

4 gelatin leaves	juice from 2-3 lemons
4 eggs	(almost 1 dl)
75 g sugar	1 dl heavy cream
grated peel of 1 lemon	

To garnish: 1 dl heavy cream for whipping

Soak the gelatin leaves in cold water for 5 minutes. (To use powdered gelatin, see the conversion table on p. 4.) Whisk the egg yolks and sugar. Whisk in the grated lemon peel together with the lemon juice.

Shake all the water from the gelatin leaves. Melt them in a double boiler and heat until lukewarm. Pour the melted gelatin in a thin stream into the egg mixture, beating the whole time.

Beat the egg whites and cream in separate bowls. First fold the egg whites into the egg mixture, then the whipped cream. Pour the mousse into a serving bowl or individual bowls. Refrigerate before serving. Garnish with whipped cream.

Rum Mousse: Use ½ to 1 dl rum instead of the lemon peel and juice.
Sherry Mousse: Use 1 dl sherry and 25 g chopped almonds instead of the lemon peel and juice.

RYE BREAD AND APPLE DESSERT
SERVES 4

In Danish this is called peasant girl with a veil, the veil being the finely grated chocolate sprinkled on this good and filling dessert.

6 dl grated dark rye bread	4-5 tbsp. jam
85 g sugar	2 ½ dl heavy cream
50 g butter	50 g finely grated chocolate
4 dl applesauce	

Mix the grated rye bread with sugar, and toast until golden with the butter on a frying pan. Cool. Place a layer of rye bread in a bowl, and top with applesauce and then with jam. Repeat, ending with a layer of rye bread. Whip the cream and cover the surface with it. Sprinkle on finely grated chocolate.

ALMOND PUDDING WITH CHERRY SAUCE
SERVES 4-5

Nothing was better than my childhood's pale yellow, quivering almond pudding with cherry sauce - though many times it was made from a mix.

½ liter light cream	5 tbsp. sugar
1 vanilla bean	7 gelatin leaves
5 egg yolks	75-100 g almonds, 3 dl heavy cream

Bring the cream to a boil with the split vanilla bean. Soak the gelatin in cold water. (To use powdered gelatin, see on p. 4.) Whisk the egg yolks together with the sugar, and beat in the boiling-hot cream. Discard the vanilla bean. Return to the pot and bring the crème almost to a boil, beating the whole time. Do not boil the crème or it will curdle. Remove the pot from the heat. Shake all water from the gelatin leaves and add them to the hot crème, beating constantly. Discard the vanilla bean and cool the crème. It will take about an hour before it begins to jell. Blanch and coarsely chop the almonds. Whip the cream. Fold the whipped cream and chopped almonds into the crème when it begins to jell. Pour it into a mold or bowl and refrigerate until completely firm.

To serve: Dip the mold or bowl quickly in boiling-hot water. Top with a serving dish and turn upside down, shaking gently to loosen the pudding. Serve with Cherry Sauce.

BREAD PUDDING
SERVES 4-5

This was a very common dessert in our grandmothers' homes. Coarse bread was especially used for porridge, while white bread was used for bread cake or pudding.

5-6 slices French bread without crust	3 eggs, 4 tbsp. sugar
40 g butter	1 vanilla bean
60 g raisins	½ liter cream or milk

Place the slices, with raisins between each layer, in a greased baking pan or dish. The top layer should be bread, butter-side up.

Beat the eggs with the sugar. Bring the milk to a boil with the split vanilla bean. Add it to the egg mixture, beating constantly. Discard the vanilla bean. Pour the mixture over the bread and raisins. Bake the pudding at 175°C for 35-40 minutes or until it has set. Serve hot or cold with berry sauce.

WINTER

(December - January - February)

Preparations for Christmas start in early December. Even though not many families slaughter their own animals, many farm families get half or whole pigs to cut up and cook. Finches made from chitterlings was one of the festive dishes served just after slaughtering time, and the dish is still popular just before Christmas. The climax of the winter months is naturally Christmas, when we eat the traditional roast duck with apples and prunes, or pork roast with crispy fat, and rice pudding or rice à l'amande. Just before the last evening of the year there is a rush to buy cod, and prices rise to astronomical heights, but luckily, cod is just as good after New Year's Eve, and much, much cheaper. Winter dishes also include yellow peas, oxtail ragout, and stewed beef, unless one is invited to a party with such fine dishes as a good roast covered with crispy fat and lemon or rum mousse. It is not as difficult to get through the dark Nordic winter when one can sit inside with good food and drink.

YELLOW PEAS
SERVES 6

This is one of the good old-fashioned soups that can be made in numerous ways, depending on the part of the country you live in. In many places on Funen and the other islands of Denmark, apples are cooked along with the peas. Today it is not necessary to soak the peas in advance since parboiled peas are available.

½ kg split (yellow) peas	½ kg potatoes
1 kg lightly salted lean pork	4 sprigs of thyme
4-5 carrots	1 large onion
½ celeriac	salt and pepper
3-4 leeks	¾ to 1 kg pork sausage

Put the peas in a pot and pour over just enough water to cover. Add the thyme and boil until the peas are tender; the cooking time varies with the variety, so check the package.

Remove the thyme and mash the peas well or force them through a sieve.

Meanwhile bring the pork to a boil with enough water to cover. Skim and add salt. Simmer the meat for about 1 hour. Add the vegetables when about 20 minutes of the cooking time is left. Add the sausage when 10 minutes is left.

Pour enough broth into the peas to give a suitable consistency - not too thin. Add the diced vegetables and season to taste.

Serve the meat and sausages with the yellow peas, with rye bread, mustard, and pickled beets on the side.

Hint: Yellow peas can also be cooked together with salted goose or duck instead of pork.

STUFFED WHOLE HEAD OF CABBAGE
SERVES 6

A large head of cabbage is more than enough to serve 6. This is a wonderful old Danish dish that has unfortunately almost been forgotten.

1 large head of cabbage
600 g ground pork and veal
3 tbsp. flour
1 large egg
1 medium onion
1 ½ dl milk or broth (bouillon)
2 tsp. salt, 1 tsp. pepper
1 tsp. dried thyme

Remove the outermost leaves from the head of cabbage. Cut a lid off the head and hollow the head out with a little pointed knife and a large spoon. Leave about 2 cm on all sides. Mix the meat with the flour and egg. Add grated onion and then the liquid, a little at a time. Season with salt, pepper, and thyme. Fill the cabbage with the mixture and put on the lid. Tie with cotton twine.

Put the stuffed head of cabbage in a pot and pour over enough water to reach half way up the head. Cover and simmer for about 1 hour.

The cabbage that was dug out of the head can be browned in a little fat in a Dutch oven. Add a little of the cabbage cooking liquid and cook until tender. Add a little cream if you like, and season with salt and pepper.

Arrange the cabbage around the stuffed head of cabbage on a platter. Hearty bread and mustard are good accompaniments.

FINCHES
SERVES 6

This dish was made just after slaughtering at the end of November or early December. It consists of various kinds of chopped variety meats and chopped pork and apples. Since it is definitely a pre-Christmas dish, ready-made finches can now be bought at the butcher's and at supermarkets in December.

2 pork hearts	a few sprigs of fresh thyme
½ kg pork liver	3 coarsely grated tart apples
2 pork kidneys	1 large onion
salt and pepper	250 g lightly salted lean pork
2 bay leaves	

Clean and rinse the meat. It is not necessary to soak the kidneys if they are rinsed well, in a vinegar and water solution if you like. Cut the meat into small pieces and cover them with water in a pot. Add salt, pepper, bay leaves, and thyme. Simmer until tender. Put the meat through a meat grinder with the peeled onion. Return to the pot and add the grated apples. Bring to a boil and season to taste.

Cut the pork into little cubes and fry them until golden and crispy on a pan. Add them to the dish just before serving.

Serve with homemade bread, pickled beets, and vinegar.

FRIED PORK
SERVES 4

This pork, fried on a pan, is served with parsley or onion sauce. You can use lightly salted fatty or lean pork.

600 g lightly salted pork

Cut the pork into 1/2-cm slices unless your butcher has already done it for you. Heat a pan well. Add the slices and fry at medium heat until the slices are light brown on both sides. Pour the melted fat from the pan as it forms or the pork will not get crispy.

Accompaniments: Boiled (new) potatoes and Parsley Sauce (see p. 37) or

Onion Sauce: Melt 3 tbsp. butter or margarine in a saucepan and simmer a couple of sliced onions in it. Stir in 3 tbsp. flour and gradually
add 4 dl milk. Boil the sauce and season with salt and white pepper.
  Hint: For a heartier dish, bread the pork slices with egg and dried
bread crumbs before frying.

Apples and Pork:
Fry the pork slices on a pan. Remove them and fry 1 kg peeled (cooking) apple wedges in the fat. Add sugar to taste. Serve the apples beside
or on top of the pork.

Sour Ribs from North Schleswig:
This is a must on Christmas lunch buffets in North Schleswig. Boil ¾
to 1 kg lean pork until tender in ¾ liter water seasoned with 1 ½ dl vinegar, 2 bay leaves, 2 whole cloves, and 5-6 whole peppercorns. Cut the
pork into slices and arrange it in overlapping layers on a platter or dish.
Skim and sieve the broth. Measure the broth and add 1 gelatin leaf per
dl broth. (To use powdered gelatin, see the conversion table on p. 4.)
Pour the mixture over the meat. Refrigerate until jelled. Serve with rye
bread and mustard.

MEAT ROLLS
SERVES 4

This Sunday dish - called legless birds in Danish - should be served with
good mashed potatoes.

¾ to 1 kg lean beef or veal, c. 8 slices
salt and pepper
8 strips pork fat (as large as your little finger)
1 medium onion, finely chopped
flour
butter or margarine for browning
3 dl water or broth (bouillon)
2 ½ dl light cream
flour for thickening
(caramel color)

Pound the meat slices gently and sprinkle with salt and pepper. Place a strip of pork fat and some of the chopped onion on each. Roll the meat and tie with cotton twine or use a skewer. Dredge in flour.

Brown the rolls on all sides in the fat in a Dutch oven. Add the water or broth, cover, and simmer for about 1 hour or until tender.

Remove the rolls from the pot and keep them hot. Add the cream. Bring to a boil and thicken. Season with salt and pepper.

Return the rolls to the sauce and heat them thoroughly before serving on a deep platter with the mashed potatoes. (See the recipe under Burning Love, p. 40.)

Pickled cucumber makes a good accompaniment.

Hint: The rolls can be filled with a little portion of spiced ground veal in addition to the strip of pork fat and seasoned with ground cloves.

STEWED BEEF
SERVES 4

The Danish name for this dish - pounded beef - comes from the days when it was necessary to pound the slices until very thin to make them tender. Today Danish beef is properly matured, so merciless pounding is no longer necessary.

¾ kg lean beef	3 medium onions
(shoulder, round, etc)	2-3 bay leaves
2-3 tbsp. flour	4 dl water or bouillon
salt and pepper	(flour for thickening)
2-3 tbsp. butter,	
margarine, or oil	

Get the butcher to cut attractive slices. Pound them lightly with the heel of your hand and dredge in a mixture of flour, salt, and pepper.

Brown the slices on both sides in the fat in a Dutch oven.

Peel and chop the onions, and brown them in the pot. Add the bay leaves and liquid.

Cover and simmer until the meat is tender, 1 to 1 ½ hours. Thicken if you like and season to taste.

Serve with mashed potatoes. (See the recipe for Burning Love, p. 40.)

ROAST BEEF WITH GLAZED ONIONS
SERVES ABOUT 12

Roast beef is party food, and the roast also has to be big enough if it is to be really good. Porterhouse makes the best large roast, while sirloin can be roasted in smaller pieces.

1 roast with a good layer of fat, 6 kg	2 carrots
salt and pepper	bouquet garni of 1 bunch of parsley,
1 to 1 ½ liters water	1 bay leaf,
2 onions	1 sprig of thyme

Slash the roast unless your butcher has done it for you. Season with salt and pepper. Brown the roast at 250°C for 15-20 minutes. Reduce the temperature to 175°C. Arrange onion wedges, sliced carrots, and the bouquet garni under the roast and pour on 1 liter of water. Continue roasting for 2 ½ to 3 hours. (Ask your butcher for advice, since the roasts thickness and shape determine the length of the roasting time.)

Remove the roast from the oven and let it stand, covered, for at least 20 minutes before carving.

Sauce: Sieve the pan drippings into a saucepan and add more broth, bouillon or water to make just under 1 ½ liters. Add a little cream (and red wine) and thicken.

Glazed Onions:
c. ¾ kg little onions (shallots have the most flavor)
75 g sugar
75 g butter

Melt the sugar until golden in a saucepan and add the butter. Add the peeled onions and brown them, stirring and shaking the pan. Cook until tender, but not mushy.

Other accompaniments: Little boiled potatoes, boiled beans and peas, pickled cucumbers.

Beef Sirloin or Short Loin: Brown a sirloin, 3 ½ to 4 kg, as above for 15 minutes, then roast for 2 hours at 160-175°C.

Monday Roast
This is obviously the rest of the Sunday roast. Allow 2 slices of roast beef per person.

250 g button mushrooms	2 ½ dl milk
2 ½ dl sauce	50 g butter
2 pickled cucumbers	salt and pepper
Mashed potatoes:	2 eggs
1 kg potatoes	pats of butter

Arrange the slices of meat in a baking dish. Fry the button mushroom slices in a little butter and arrange them over the meat. Chop the pickled cucumbers and add them to the sauce. Boil and mash the potatoes. Add the butter and milk, and finally whisk in the eggs. Spread the mashed potatoes over the meat and sauce and top with pats of butter. Bake at 200°C for 20-30 minutes.

OXTAIL RAGOUT
SERVES 6

This filling winter dish tastes just as good the day after - perhaps even better. It is important to cook the oxtails until very tender so that the meat can easily be removed from the bone with a fork.

2 oxtails	3 tbsp. tomato paste
2-3 tbsp. flour	4-5 dl broth or bouillon
4-5 tbsp. butter	(from a cube)
2-3 onions	1-2 bay leaves
½ celeriac	a couple of sprigs of thyme
4-5 carrots	salt and pepper
3-4 leeks	(flour for thickening)
2-3 tsp. paprika	

Ask your butcher to cut the oxtails into segments. Peel and slice the onions. Peel and dice the celeriac and carrots. Slice the leeks. Dredge the oxtail pieces in flour and brown them in the fat in a Dutch oven.

Add the onions and brown them. Add the paprika and tomato paste, diluted with a little bouillon. Add the rest of the liquid and the spices.

Cover and simmer for 1 hour. Add the vegetables and cook until everything is tender. The meat should be so tender that it almost falls from the bones. Season to taste and thicken if you like. Serve in a deep platter and sprinkle with chopped parsley.

The classical Danish accompaniment is mashed potatoes or *potato snow* - mealy boiled potatoes forced through a potato ricer direct onto the serving dish.

Hint: You can add 250 g button mushrooms sautéed with butter or a little dry sherry just before serving.

PORK ROAST WITH CRACKLING
SERVES 8

Pork roast is winter and Christmas food. You can use pork neck or ham, whole, boned, or cut into smaller pieces. Until recently, slaughtering methods made it difficult for cooks to get the fat crispy. But now butchers realize that people want crackling that really crackles, and meat that tastes the way it used to. Todays slaughtering methods are better, and new strains have juicier, more tender meat.

1 pork neck or 1 piece of ham	*Sauce:*
(2 ½ to 3 kg)	7-8 dl broth/bouillon and
salt and pepper	pan juices
bay leaves	1 dl cream
1 liter water or bouillon	flour for thickening
2 onions	(caramel color)
2-3 carrots	salt and pepper
2-3 celery stalks	

Get your butcher to make deep slits in the roast. Rub with salt and pepper. Make sure to get the salt into the slits so that the crackling gets crispy. Put the roast on a rack over a baking pan and brown for 15 minutes at 250°C. Reduce the temperature to 175°C and pour the water (bouillon) into the pan; add the cut carrots, chopped onions and celery. Roast for 1 ¼ hours if you use a pork neck and 2-3 hours for a whole boned ham.

Let the roast stand for 15-20 minutes before carving.

Meanwhile, pour the drippings from the pan. Skim off all fat and sieve it. Pour the juices into a saucepan and dilute with bouillon or broth, making 8 dl in all. Add cream and bring to a boil. Thicken and season to taste.

Slice the roast and serve with boiled/glazed potatoes and Red Cabbage. (See the recipe under Roast Duck, p. 62.)

ROAST DUCK WITH PRUNES AND APPLES
SERVES 4-5

Only use a duck that weighs 3 kg (dressed). It is still possible to get a good, meaty duck at the butcher's, though supermarket ducks have been something of a disappointment in recent years. Danish Christmas duck naturally has to be filled with apples and prunes, and served with the traditional glazed potatoes and red cabbage. Though you can buy red cabbage, it really must be homemade for Christmas.

1 duck, c. 3 kg (dressed)
salt and pepper
c. 250 g pitted prunes
3-4 aromatic cooking apples
1 onion
2 carrots
a sprig of thyme

Sauce:
6 dl broth made from the wings,
neck, giblets, etc.
a little salt
drippings

Dry the inside of the duck with a paper towel and rub with salt and pepper. Fill the duck with peeled apple wedges and prunes and close with a skewer or sew with cotton twine. Pull the neck skin over the back and fasten with a skewer. Dry the outside well to make sure it turns crispy during roasting.

Place the duck upside down on a rack over a baking pan. Brown it at 250°C for 15 minutes. Turn and brown for another 15 minutes.

Reduce the temperature to 175°C and sprinkle on salt and pepper. Pour the fat from the pan and add water, together with the quartered onion, sliced carrots, and thyme. Roast for 1 ¾ hours. Meanwhile, boil the wings, neck, giblets, etc. with a small quartered onion, sliced celery, and thyme.

Remove the duck from the oven and pour off the drippings. Let the drippings stand for a moment and skim off the fat.

Sauce: Pour the drippings into a little saucepan together with the sieved broth, 6 dl in all. Thicken and season to taste.

You can brown the duck at 250°C for 10-15 minutes with the oven vent open. Let the duck stand for at least 15 minutes before carving.

Homemade red cabbage:
1 red cabbage, finely chopped
4 tbsp. butter
1 dl wine vinegar

2 dl red currant juice
(a little sugar)
salt

Heat the fat in a pot until golden. Add the cabbage and mix. Add the wine vinegar and red currant juice and season with salt (and sugar). Cover and simmer for 1 hour. Stir frequently so that the cabbage does not stick.

Glazed Potatoes: Melt 85 g sugar on a pan until golden. Add 75 g butter. Rinse 1 kg little boiled, peeled potatoes under cold water. Drain. Glaze and brown them on the hot pan with the caramelized sugar, turning constantly.

A good accompaniment to Christmas duck is apples, cut in half, filled with red or black currant or rowanberry jelly and steamed.

RICE PORRIDGE
SERVES 4

Porridge was one of the main dishes in Denmark for centuries, and in our grandmothers' time it was on the menu once or twice a week. Rice Porridge was initially a festive dish, though it later became common weekday fare. Rice porridge is still the first course at Christmas dinner in many Danish families.

2 liters whole milk
225 g short-grained rice
½ tsp. salt

Accompaniments:
Sugar and cinnamon
butter

Bring the milk to a boil in a thick-bottomed saucepan. Add the rice gradually, stirring constantly. Bring to a boil and simmer for about 45 minutes. Stir frequently to prevent the porridge from sticking. Remove the pot from the heat and stir in the salt.

Mix the sugar and cinnamon. Serve the porridge piping hot with the sugar and cinnamon mixture and a pat of butter.

Hint: According to old Danish traditions, berry juice or sweet beer is served with rice porridge. If the porridge is made with skim milk, remember that it will stick to the pot more easily.

RICE CAKES
SERVES 4

Rice porridge made from ½ liter whole milk and ¾ dl short-grained rice.

1 large egg	1 tbsp. sugar
3 tbsp. flour	grated lemon peel
1 dl milk	

Accompaniment: Powdered sugar or syrup
jam

Make porridge from the milk and rice. Cool, and mix in the egg together with the flour, milk, sugar, and grated lemon peel. Fry little cakes in fat on a pan.

Serve immediately with powdered sugar or syrup and jam.

RICE À L'AMANDE
SERVES 4

In spite of its French-sounding name, this dessert is unknown in France. In Denmark it has become a tradition to serve it on Christmas Eve.

1 portion of rice porridge made from 1 liter milk and 125 g rice
2-3 tbsp. sugar
seeds of 1 vanilla bean
½ dl sweet sherry or port
50 g blanched, coarsely chopped almonds
3 dl heavy cream

Mix the sugar and seeds scraped from the vanilla bean into the cold rice porridge. Mix in the wine and the chopped almonds. Whip the cream and fold it in. Refrigerate before serving. Serve with Cherry Sauce.

Cherry Sauce
½ kg canned stoned cherries in their syrup
1 to 1 ½ tsp. potato flour

Put the cherries and their syrup in a saucepan and bring to a boil. Dissolve the potato flour in a little water. Pour it into the boiling-hot liquid, stirring constantly. Do not boil the sauce after you add the potato flour or it will be stringy.

INDEX